Overwatch
Beginner's Guide

1st Century Skills **INNOVATION LIBRARY**

Josh Gregory

CHERRY LAKE PRESS

Published in the United States of America by Cherry Lake Publishing Group
Ann Arbor, Michigan
www.cherrylakepublishing.com

Reading Adviser: Beth Walker Gambro, MS, Ed., Reading Consultant, Yorkville, IL

Cherry Lake Press is an imprint of Cherry Lake Publishing Group.

Library of Congress Cataloging-in-Publication Data

Names: Gregory, Josh, author.
Title: Overwatch : beginner's guide / by Josh Gregory.
Description: Ann Arbor, Michigan : Cherry Lake Publishing, 2023. | Series: Unofficial guides | Includes bibliographical
   references and index. | Audience: Grades 4-6 | Summary: "The latest in a long line of megahit games from Blizzard
   Entertainment, Overwatch quickly became a big part of the esports world upon its 2016 release. With the 2022 addition
   of Overwatch 2 to the mix, more players than ever are jumping in to find out what makes the game so fun. This book
   gives readers all the information they need to start winning matches online. Includes table of contents, author biography,
   sidebars, glossary, index, and informative backmatter"— Provided by publisher.
Identifiers: LCCN 2023002158 (print) | LCCN 2023002159 (ebook) | ISBN 9781668927977 (library binding) |
   ISBN 9781668929025 (paperback) | ISBN 9781668930496 (epub) | ISBN 9781668933459 (kindle edition) |
   ISBN 9781668931974 (pdf)
Subjects: LCSH: Overwatch (Video game)—Juvenile literature. | Fantasy games—Juvenile literature.
Classification: LCC GV1469.37 .G746 2023 (print) | LCC GV1469.37 (ebook) | DDC 794.8—dc23/eng/20230228
LC record available at https://lccn.loc.gov/2023002158
LC ebook record available at https://lccn.loc.gov/2023002159

Cherry Lake Publishing Group would like to acknowledge the work of the Partnership for 21st Century Learning,
a Network of Battelle for Kids. Please visit http://www.battelleforkids.org/networks/p21 for more information.

Printed in the United States of America

Note from publisher: Websites change regularly, and their future contents are outside of our control.
Supervise children when conducting any recommended online searches for extended learning opportunities.

Josh Gregory is the author of more than 200 books for kids. He has written about everything from animals to technology to history. A graduate of the University of Missouri–Columbia, he currently lives in Chicago, Illinois.

Contents

CHAPTER 1

Creating a Classic

If you're interested in video games, you probably already know a few things about *Overwatch*. Since its release in 2016, it has consistently been among the most popular competitive online games in the world. Every month, millions of people log in to play the game. Huge audiences gather on Twitch and other services to watch their favorite streamers in action. There's even a professional **esports** league devoted entirely to the game—*Overwatch* League, with teams located in major cities throughout the United States, Canada, China, and South Korea.

Overwatch is a **first-person** shooter where teams each compete to complete **objectives** such as taking control of points on a map or escorting a vehicle safely from one location to another. At the start of a match, each player chooses a different character, or hero, to play as. Each hero has different strengths, weaknesses, and abilities, much like the playable characters in MOBA games such as *League of Legends* or *Dota 2*. This unique combination of MOBA and first-person shooter gameplay has helped *Overwatch* stand out from other competitive team-based games.

The huge variety of playable heroes in *Overwatch* is one of the game's most unique features.

Overwatch was created by the **developers** at Blizzard Entertainment. Prior to *Overwatch*, Blizzard had already become famous for creating hugely successful games such as *World of Warcraft, StarCraft,* and *Diablo*. Because its previous games have all been such major hits, there are always high expectations when Blizzard announces a new project. So, when *Overwatch* was officially revealed to the public in November 2014 at the annual BlizzCon event, fans couldn't wait to get their hands on the game.

They got their first chance about a year later, when Blizzard begin inviting players to help **beta test** the game. Players lucky enough to get access to the beta got the chance to try the game before anyone else. Word of mouth began to spread: Blizzard had created another classic.

Upon its official release in 2016, *Overwatch* received heavy praise from critics and players alike. Many have ranked it among the greatest video games ever made, and it quickly became one of the most popular games in the esports community.

Like any successful online game in recent years, *Overwatch* received regular updates as time went on. By adding new heroes for players to try, rebalancing the game to prevent any one hero from being more

Ramattra was added to the game in December 2022, more than eight years after the launch of *Overwatch*.

powerful than others, and adding new **cosmetic** items, Blizzard was able to keep players interested in the game for years after its release. But eventually, the developers decided they needed to try something even bigger to draw more players.

In November 2019, at that year's BlizzCon, Blizzard announced that it was working on *Overwatch 2*. But this sequel would not be like most video game sequels.

The *Overwatch* menu screen changes frequently, depending on the latest additions to the game.

KIRIKO ⊕

FILTER

👕 SKINS 0/7	＞
😊 EMOTES 0/5	＞
✌ VICTORY POSES 0/3	＞
⛰ HIGHLIGHT INTROS 0/5	＞
⬛ SOUVENIRS 0/36	＞
🔫 WEAPON CHARMS 2/54	＞
🗋 SPRAYS 2/339	＞
🎤 VOICE LINES 0/18	＞
💥 WEAPONS 0/1	＞

HERO INFORMATION

HERO CHALLENGES

ENTER CHAT

ESC BACK

The release of *Overwatch 2* saw the addition of Kiriko to the hero roster.

The first *Overwatch* was released as a standard paid package: players paid a one-time fee for full access to the game. But *Overwatch 2* would follow in the footsteps of free-to-play games like *Fortnite* and *Apex Legends*. Anyone can download these games and play them for free, but dedicated players can purchase cosmetics, new heroes, and other add-ons through **microtransactions**.

A New Kind of Storytelling

Unlike many similar games, *Overwatch* did not come with any kind of single-player story mode. Despite this, the game's storyline and characters have become two of its most popular features among some fans. How could this be possible in a game with no story mode?

Soon after the release of the first *Overwatch*, Blizzard began releasing short animated films set in the game's world. These help flesh out the back stories of the many hero characters and explain why they are battling each other. There are also *Overwatch* comic books, novels, and other media based on the game. Each of these reveals new details about the series' story.

Because the story of *Overwatch* is told almost entirely outside the game itself, many players enjoy the competitive aspects of the game without ever paying attention to the story. But for others, it has become one of the most exciting parts of the series.

Released in October 2022, *Overwatch 2* contained all the heroes and maps of the first game along with some new content. It completely replaced the original *Overwatch*, which can no longer be played. Blizzard plans to regularly add new features to the game, including a new mode where teams of players can face off against computer-controlled enemies.

But in the meantime, *Overwatch 2* is a lot like the first *Overwatch*—except now it's free! It's the perfect opportunity for new players to join in the fun.

Whether you're a new player jumping into the action with *Overwatch 2* or an experienced veteran, there is always something new to learn about this unique game. Are you ready to get started?

If you are new to *Overwatch*, try the training mode, where the popular hero Tracer will teach you the basics of the game.

CHAPTER 2

Mastering the Basics

Getting started with *Overwatch* is easy. All you need is a current video game console or a gaming PC. You can download *Overwatch 2* for free through your console's online store or through Blizzard's Battle.net service if you're playing on a PC.

Once you've downloaded the game, you can jump straight into your first match if you like. But if you're new to *Overwatch*, it's probably a good idea to try out the game's training mode first. This will introduce you to the basic controls of the game and give you some space to practice without the pressure of human opponents trying to defeat you.

The general controls of *Overwatch* will probably be familiar if you've ever played a first-person shooter before. You'll be able to run, jump, crouch, and aim and fire your weapon. There are also basic commands that let you communicate with your teammates at the press of a button. The most important of these is the "ping" system. By aiming at various locations, players, and objects in the game and pressing a couple of buttons, you can send valuable messages to your teammates. For example, you might aim at an enemy

Competitive mode is where most serious players spend their time, but Unranked mode is a good choice if you are still learning.

The ping system makes it easy to communicate quickly without using voice chat.

player and double-tap the ping button. This will tell your teammates where the enemy is, allowing them to avoid attacks and get the jump on the opposing player.

The rest of *Overwatch*'s controls depend on which hero you are using. Each hero has a different set of abilities, and choosing different heroes has a huge impact on what you'll need to do to succeed in a match. Heroes are divided into three categories: tank, support, and damage per second (DPS).

Tank heroes have abilities that are designed to absorb damage and protect teammates from incoming attacks. Their role is to guard the other players during a match and escort them to where they need to be.

Support heroes mostly have abilities that can heal or **buff** teammates, making them more powerful. Some also have abilities that can debuff opponents, or make them weaker. These heroes do not generally focus on attacking directly.

Staying Safe

Like most online games, *Overwatch* has players teaming up with and facing off against strangers from all over the world. While it's important to stay in contact with your teammates during a match, be sure to stick to discussing only the game if you are on voice chat. Don't talk about yourself, your personal life, or your friends and family.

Generally, it's best to avoid voice chat altogether if you aren't playing with real-life friends. Instead, use the game's built-in "ping" system to alert your teammates to important things during a match. It's faster, and you don't need to talk at all.

DPS heroes are the main attackers in *Overwatch*. Their abilities are focused on doing damage to opponents as quickly as possible. That's why it is known as the "damage per second" category. This might seem like the most straightforward role if you are used to other first-person shooters. However, playing as a DPS can be tough—you will be a main target for opposing players, and your teammates will really be relying on you to do damage and push forward.

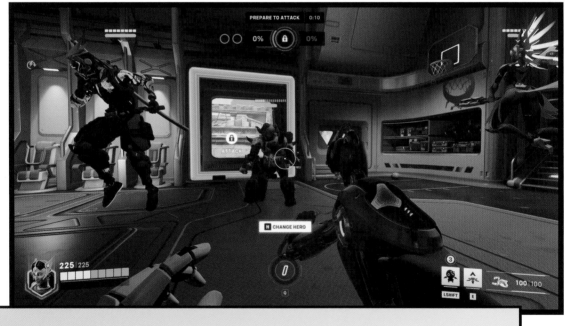

Each match will begin with you and your teammates gathered behind a door as a timer counts down.

In the original *Overwatch*, teams were each made up of six players. But *Overwatch 2* made the switch to five-player teams. Each team is composed of two support heroes, two DPS, and one tank. When you join a match, you will have to decide whether you want to play as support, DPS, or tank. You can switch heroes during a match, but you will need to stay within the category you picked.

Once you've joined a match and chosen your hero, your team will start off grouped together in your home base. A countdown will begin to let you know when the match is going to kick off. Once the countdown ends, you will probably see your teammates rush out of the home base area toward the objective marked on your screen.

Working with your team to complete objectives is the main focus in *Overwatch*—not simply defeating opponents. When you select quick play or competitive modes in *Overwatch*, which are the main game modes, each match will cycle between four different game types: Assault, Control, Escort, and Hybrid. Each of these game types has different types of objectives. In Assault, teams battle to take over and protect different points on the map. Once a team takes control of two points, the match ends.

In Control, teams battle over a single control point. During the time a team has control of the point, a meter will increase toward 100 percent. Once a team fills their meter, the round ends, and once a team wins two rounds, they win the match.

In Escort, one team's objective is to protect a vehicle as it moves across the map. The team's players need to be near the vehicle to keep it moving. The other team's objective is to stop them by defeating them and keeping them away from the vehicle until a timer runs down.

When you have an Escort goal, you will need to stay near an object to keep it moving forward.

When you have an Attack goal, simply head toward
the indicated point and prepare for battle.

Finally, Hybrid combines Assault with Escort. First, teams
will battle over a control point. Then, the winner of
this battle must escort a vehicle from that point to
a different location on the map.

At first, this might seem like a lot to take in. But the
game will clearly mark your objectives, and once you
play a few rounds you should get the hang of the
basic flow of a match. You will also start to learn the
layouts of the game's maps.

CHAPTER 3

Getting Competitive

It's tough to succeed at *Overwatch* without specializing. For some players, this means sticking to playing a certain role—tank, support, or DPS. For others, it means focusing on a small handful of heroes. If you're just starting out, give a bunch of heroes and roles a try to see what seems most fun to you. Then pick one to focus on for a while. Don't overthink your decision. You can always learn new heroes later.

Once you have a hero you want to learn, try to play as that character as often as possible. Each one is completely unique, and playing as one hero is often a completely different experience from playing as another. Learn how each of your hero's weapons and abilities work. Each hero has a different main weapon. These can range from long-range lasers to close-up blades. Unlike in many first-person shooters, you cannot pick up new weapons in levels—you have to use the ones that come with your hero.

When trying a new character, be sure to check out their weapons and abilities to see what sets them apart from other heroes.

Many heroes have abilities that help them move around the map in different ways. For example, some characters can quickly dash to avoid attacks and get in close, while others can fly. Some characters have healing abilities, while others can deploy shields. Some have extra-powerful attacks, or abilities that let them aim more easily or lock onto opponents.

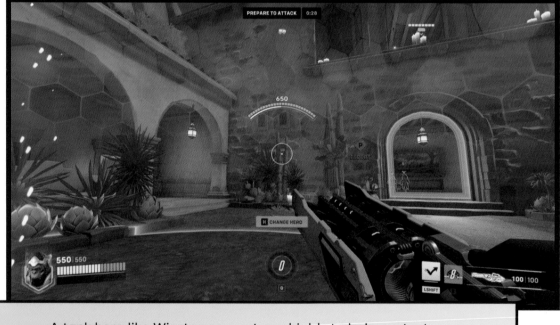

A tank hero like Winston can put up shields to help protect against enemy attacks.

You can see cooldown timers in the bottom-right corner of the screen.

Each ability aside from a character's main attack is on a cooldown timer. This means you have to wait a few seconds after using an ability before using it again. Learning how to use your abilities at the right times is crucial. You don't want to be caught in a situation where you need an ability but you already used it and need to wait for the cooldown.

Watching the Pros

Because *Overwatch* is such a successful, long-running game, there are a lot of experienced, skilled players out there. Many of them regularly stream their matches online. These can be a lot of fun to watch—you'll see incredible action and tense matches where a last-minute play can help a team come from behind. But watching the pros stream is more than just a good time. It's also one of the best ways to learn advanced strategies for the game.

As you watch, pay close attention to how skilled players use different heroes' abilities in different situations. Watch how they move around the game's maps to get the jump on their opponents. Observe how they work together with their teammates. Do teams use specific combinations of heroes to battle more effectively? How do they assist each other throughout a match? The more you watch, the more you'll learn. Then you just need to practice until you can pull off the trickiest strategies even when you're under pressure.

Each hero also has an ultimate ability. This is a very powerful ability that can only be used after charging up the character's ultimate meter to 100 percent. This meter will slowly rise as you play, and it will rise faster as you attack opponents or heal teammates. As with other abilities, timing is everything when it comes to ultimates. Save these powerful moves for just the right moment and you can quickly turn the tide of a match.

When the icon at the bottom center of the screen is lit up like this, it's time to let loose with your ultimate ability.

CHAPTER 4

Skin Deep

For many players, a big part of the fun of *Overwatch* is in customizing their characters with unlockable cosmetic items. These come in several different categories. Skins are different appearances you can assign to each of the game's heroes. Emotes are short animations you can activate for your hero in the middle of a match. You can also do things like change the colors of your weapons, add decorative charms to your weapons, or change the celebratory pose your character does after winning a match.

So how do you unlock new cosmetics to try? One way is to visit the in-game shop, which is accessible from the main menu. Here, you'll find a rotating assortment of cosmetic items that are available for purchase as microtransactions. Simply choose the cosmetic you want and purchase it to unlock it forever. The items available in the shop change frequently, and some are only available for a limited time.

The other main way to unlock new cosmetics is to level up your in-game Battle Pass. As you play *Overwatch*, you will earn points called XP for doing everything from

The items for sale in the in-game shop change all the time.

winning matches to pulling off specific techniques in battle. Once you get enough XP, you will increase the Battle Pass level by one. Each level will unlock a new cosmetic item. There are two versions of the Battle Pass: a free one and a paid one. The paid one will give you more items, and it also increases the amount of XP you receive.

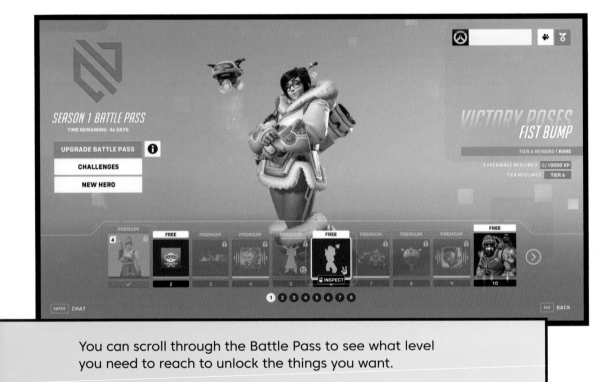

You can scroll through the Battle Pass to see what level you need to reach to unlock the things you want.

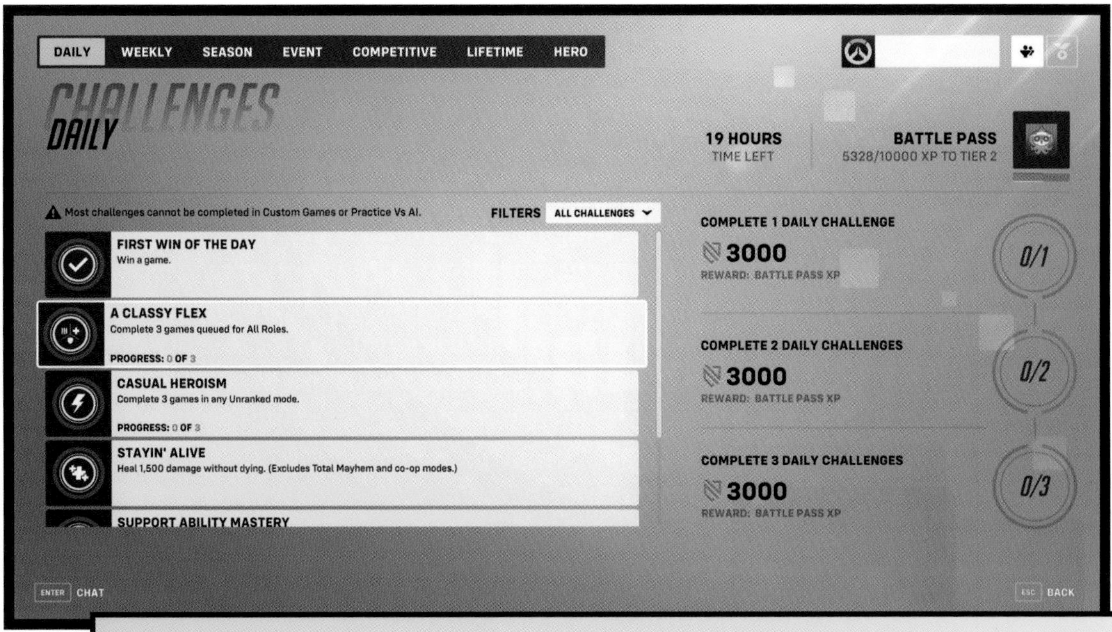
DAILY
WEEKLY
SEASON
EVENT
COMPETITIVE
LIFETIME
HERO
CHALLENGES
DAILY
19 HOURS
TIME LEFT
BATTLE PASS
5328/10000 XP TO TIER 2
Most challenges cannot be completed in Custom Games or Practice Vs AI.
FILTERS
ALL CHALLENGES
FIRST WIN OF THE DAY
Win a game.
A CLASSY FLEX
Complete 3 games queued for All Roles.
PROGRESS: 0 OF 3
CASUAL HEROISM
Complete 3 games in any Unranked mode.
PROGRESS: 0 OF 3
STAYIN' ALIVE
Heal 1,500 damage without dying. (Excludes Total Mayhem and co-op modes.)
SUPPORT ABILITY MASTERY
COMPLETE 1 DAILY CHALLENGE
3000
REWARD: BATTLE PASS XP
0/1
COMPLETE 2 DAILY CHALLENGES
3000
REWARD: BATTLE PASS XP
0/2
COMPLETE 3 DAILY CHALLENGES
3000
REWARD: BATTLE PASS XP
0/3
ENTER CHAT
ESC BACK

Completing challenges is the fastest way to level up your Battle Pass and unlock new items.

Want to increase your XP as quickly as possible? Try completing challenges as you play. Challenges are special tasks that you can complete to earn extra XP. For example, a challenge might ask you to knock out a certain number of opponents without being knocked out yourself. New challenges will pop up every day. Some need to be completed that day. Others give you a week or even longer to complete them. You can check your progress and see which challenges are available by selecting “Challenges” from the main menu.

Watch Your Wallet

In games with microtransactions, it can be easier than you might think to end up spending too much money. Even though each skin or other item might only cost a few dollars, these transactions can really start to add up. When you are playing *Overwatch* or any game with microtransactions, be sure to set a budget for your spending and stick to it. And always be sure to get permission from a parent or guardian before spending any money at all.

To see what you've unlocked so far and customize your heroes, select "Heroes" from the main *Overwatch 2* menu. Then choose which hero you'd like to customize. You'll see a list of all the available skins, emotes, and other cosmetics available for that hero. The ones you've purchased or unlocked will be available to equip. The others will have prices next to them so you can decide whether or not you want to purchase them.

Overwatch is a deep, complex game, and there is always something new to learn—even for experienced players. But now that you understand the basics, the rest will come with practice and experience. Get out there and start competing. Soon enough, you'll be climbing the ranks of the online leaderboards. Good luck!

Express your creativity by customizing your favorite heroes.

GLOSSARY

beta test (BAY-tuh TEST) a final test before releasing a video game, sometimes conducted by inviting fans to try a game before it is officially released

buff (BUHF) to temporarily strengthen a character's abilities in a game

cosmetic (kahz-MEH-tik) relating to how something looks

developers (dih-VEL-uh-purz) people who make video games or other computer programs

esports (EE-sports) organized, professional video game competitions

first-person (FURST-PUR-sun) taking place through the eyes of a character

microtransactions (MYE-kroh-trans-ak-shuhns) things that can be purchased for a small amount of money within a video game or other computer program

objectives (uhb-JEK-tivs) goals

FIND OUT MORE

Books

Gregory, Josh. *Careers in Esports*. Ann Arbor, MI: Cherry Lake Publishing, 2021.

Loh-Hagan, Virginia. *Video Games. In the Know: Influencers and Trends*. Ann Arbor, MI: 45th Parallel Press, 2021.

Orr, Tamra. *Video Sharing. Global Citizens: Social Media*. Ann Arbor, MI: Cherry Lake Press, 2019.

Reeves, Diane Lindsey. *Do You Like Getting Creative? Career Clues for Kids*. Ann Arbor, MI: Cherry Lake Press, 2023.

Websites

With an adult, learn more online with these suggested searches.

Overwatch 2
Check out the official *Overwatch* website for the latest updates on the game.

Overwatch Wiki
This fan-made website offers in-depth info on every aspect of the *Overwatch* series, from gameplay tips to story details.

INDEX